PRAISE FOR *THE WORRIED WELL*

The poems in *The Worried Well* are beautifully built, rigged with wonder and oomph. I never knew what to expect on each page—the poems ripple with deadpan humor, quicksilver thinking, shrewd leaps, and cinematic excitements. Language, here, is malleable and splendid. Subjects are wide-ranging: a green couch, death, matryoshka dolls, bus stops, money, and Narcissus at a pharmacy. Imagination, here, is splendid and malleable. These poems renew my faith in poetry, in its ability to infuse the familiar with new sensations.

—**Eduardo C. Corral**, Prize Judge and author of *Guillotine*

In *The Worried Well*, anxiety takes the form of a dybbuk, the malevolent spirit from Jewish mythology who possesses and torments the living. But that spirit doesn't stop at anxiety. It surfaces again and again throughout these finely wrought yet agitated poems, arising here in chronic illness and debt, there in fascists and shame, in pride, in a grandfather's death. The world of Anthony Immergluck's poems, no matter how rooted in significant pain and chaos, is a scrutinized world—and scrutiny requires distance. That distance comes across in biting humor, keen self-awareness, allusions ranging from the Old Testament to *E.T.*, and the depth of clarity that arises from art's necessary curations. Only from that perspective could we get such a fine image as "the sun that sucks the wet from figs," or one of my new favorite metaphors: "Debt is a splintering pillory. / A lifetime of little deaths." And only after all this distance could a speaker ultimately proclaim, "When your hot breath finds my chest / [. . .] it feels so much like stealing."

—**Corey Van Landingham**, author of *Reader, I*

The poems in *The Worried Well* are magical in their notions and totally everyday in their locations, while throughout the imagination is going full bore with material that in lesser hands could be maudlin. Illness, doubts, crying on the red-eye—so much of what Immergluck shows us is our own everyday lives, but through a twisting kaleidoscope where the body is a world and you spend too much time in the hospital and where watching *The Fellowship of the Ring* with Grandpa near the end of his life is simultaneously the funniest and saddest thing you could ever do. These are great poems written in a panoply of voices you don't expect, but they always seem just right. I marveled, and laughed aloud, at these poems.

—**Matthew Rohrer, author of** *The Sky Contains the Plans*

THE WORRIED WELL

Thank you to the following journals, in which poems from this collection were originally published, occasionally in different forms:

Arkansas International: "In a Tent"
Beloit Poetry Journal: "Bus Stops," "Narcissus at the Pharmacy," and "Woo"
Copper Nickel: "Work" and "Worry (the Dybbuk)"
Driftwood Press: "Utopia"
Emrys Journal: "Afterlife" and "Heroin, Pt. 1"
Grist: "Social Studies"
Harpur Palate: "Deadsong"
Moon City Review: "A City Without Money"
Narrative: "David Comes Home" and "Mise en Place"
Nimrod International Journal: "Better," "Burden of Care," and "Matryoshka"
Pleiades: "Caution!"
Rumble Fish Quarterly: "Suicidal in Paradise"
Rust & Moth: "The Metaphor Game"
Sequestrum: "Green Couch," "Halfway," "In Quarantine," "The New House," and "The Old House"
Sonora Review: "Surgeries"
Tahoma Literary Review: "Two Fathers"
The Blue Mountain Review: "The Museum of Hospital Art"
TriQuarterly: "Of My Fictions"

The Slowdown featured "Worry (the Dybbuk)."

THE WORRIED WELL

POEMS

WINNER OF THE 2024 AUTUMN HOUSE
RISING WRITER PRIZE

ANTHONY IMMERGLUCK

PITTSBURGH

The Worried Well
Copyright © 2025 by Anthony Immergluck
ISBN: 978-1-63768-103-9
Published by Autumn House Press
All Rights Reserved

Cover Art: *From the Tomb*, watercolor and gouache on paper,
    by Marci Washington, courtesy of Rena Bransten Gallery
Book and Cover Design: Mike Corrao
Author Photo: Anthony Immergluck

Library of Congress Cataloging-in-Publication Data

Names: Immergluck, Anthony, author.
Title: The worried well / Anthony Immergluck.
Description: Pittsburgh : Autumn House Press, 2025.
Identifiers: LCCN 2024048373 (print) | LCCN 2024048374 (ebook) | ISBN
    9781637681039 (paperback) | ISBN 9781637681060 (epub)
Subjects: LCGFT: Poetry.
Classification: LCC PS3609.M59 W67 2025 (print) | LCC PS3609.M59 (ebook)
    | DDC 811/.6--dc23/eng/20241023
LC record available at https://lccn.loc.gov/2024048373
LC ebook record available at https://lccn.loc.gov/2024048374

Printed in the United States on acid-free paper that meets the international standards of permanent books intended for purchase by libraries.

No part of this book can be reproduced in any form whatsoever without prior written permission from the publisher, except in the case of brief quotations embodied in critical reviews or essays. Without in any way limiting the author's exclusive rights under copyright, any use of this publication to "train" generative artificial intelligence (AI) technologies to generate text is expressly prohibited. The author reserves all rights to license uses of this work for generative AI training and development of machine learning language models. For information about permission to reprint, write us at Autumn House Press, 5614 Elgin Street, Pittsburgh, PA 15206, or email us at info@autumnhouse.org.

Autumn House Press is a nonprofit corporation whose mission is the publication and promotion of poetry and other fine literature. The press gratefully acknowledges support from individual donors, public and private foundations, and government agencies. This book was supported, in part, by the Greater Pittsburgh Arts Council and the Pennsylvania Council on the Arts, a state agency funded by the Commonwealth of Pennsylvania.

For Grandpa, who always said my poetry would make me a millionaire, and Grandma, who always said I'd be broke but I'd be happy.

CONTENTS

PART 1: THE WORRY

I. THE DYBBUK	3
Worry (the Dybbuk)	5
Goliath	7
Deadsong	8
Narcissus at the Pharmacy	12
The Metaphor Game	14
Utopia	15
Social Studies, Pt. 1	16
Caution!	19
Burden of Care	20
Suicidal in Paradise	22
Red-Eye	24
II. SO LONG MY BOY AND BE CAREFULL	25
Surgeries	27
The Museum of Hospital Art	29
Ten Things I Love About Visiting You in the Hospital	31
Watching *The Fellowship of the Ring* with Grandpa Near the End of His Life	33
So Long My Boy and Be Carefull	34
Braver	36
The Weight	37
Afterlife	38
So Long My Boy and Be Carefull	39
Of My Fictions	41
Woo	43
So Long My Boy and Be Carefull	45
Two Fathers	47
Lifebed	49

PART 2: THE WELL

I. Cohabitations — 53

- The Old House — 55
- Social Studies, Pt. 2 — 57
- Chicago in Winter — 60
- Green Couch — 62
- In a Tent — 64
- To the Spiders, I Whisper: — 66
- Indefinitely — 67
- Mise en Place — 69
- Halfway — 73
- In Fidelity — 75
- In Quarantine — 77
- The New House — 78

II. The Golem — 81

- Better — 83
- Two Sons — 85
- Bus Stops — 86
- Heroin, Pt. 1 — 90
- A City Without Money — 93
- Matryoshka — 95
- The Golem — 96
- Closing Up Shop — 98
- Work — 100
- Hating My Baby — 101
- David Comes Home — 103

Acknowledgments — 107

PART I

THE WORRY

I. THE DYBBUK

WORRY (THE DYBBUK)

I have a worry mother and
I have a worry father and
once they shared a worry and
my own worry, a sprout in
this worry dirt, bullied by
the worry weeds, spoiled by
the worry sun and rain and
I the runt among a litter of
suckling worries and the
worry is the current and
we are its conductors and
the worry is the currency we
interchange on holidays and
the worry is the ribbon of
rot running deep in the
center of a chestnut and
my worry and another
worry said *I do* to worry and
we warm our tea with
worry and we wonder if
there ever was and ever
could be a home with
no worry chewing through
the attic and we wonder how
a shoulder might shoulder un-
burdened by this dybbuk and
I worry that were we to
land on an island without
worry our worries would
starve or worse, survive
on one another's offal and
I worry that the worry is
the best of us after all

I only ever held a worry
hand and I only ever ate
a worry pastry and I don't
know why I told a worry
child not to worry when
surely the trick is to give
the worry a name and then
to call it again and again.

GOLIATH

I have been Goliath,
    toppled like a soufflé
from a pebble to the temple.

In the sun that sucks the wet from figs,
    I have wilted and wondered

how I have been the mammoth
    bowing to the javelin.

The redwood besotted
    and felled by rot.

All my life, I have been bested
by such small and helpless things.

DEADSONG

I.

I will die in a gasping panic
with plastic in my windpipe.

II.

I will die in a rat king
of shrapnel and rubber,
piecemeal by the interstate.

(It will be my fault—
I do get moony.)

III.

I will die trying to fix
a household appliance
I do not understand.

IV.

I will die the way my father
says I will: trying to pet some
wild and cornered creature.

V.

I will die the way my mother
says I will: famous and ancient,
painless in my sleep.

VI.

I will die upon the hatchet
of a charismatic maniac.

(I am always inviting
vampires inside.)

VII.

I will die from a benzo overdose,
which I'm told is uncommon.

(Cessation is worse.)

VIII.

I will die concussed and
bloody on the half-pipe.

(I am too old to ollie but
the urge is only growing.)

IX.

I will die digesting
the silica packet
from a bag of trail mix.

(I gobble by the fistful.
I do not pay attention.)

X.

I will die in the desert,
molting like a cicada.

(I will not remember
how I got there. I will
try to drink the sand.)

XI.

I will die when the mole I'm told
to monitor goes melanoma
and the melanoma goes supernova
as it did for all the stars that made me.

(I am building a guest
room for the cancer.)

XII.

I will die early in the fracas
when the fascists snap
their tethers.

(I'm a partisan, to be sure,
but I am easily outrun.)

XIII.

I will die, uninsured,
of a curable malady.

(Debt is a splintering pillory.
A lifetime of little deaths.)

XIV.

I will die the way that men do,
barnacled with secrets,
having never apologized.

XV.

I will die the way young
soldiers and young
poets often do.

(No one has to ask.)

XVI.

I will die of shame
at a cocktail party.

(My solar plexus tells
me this is possible.)

XVII.

I will die at sea,
reefing the mainsail
to balance the tempest.

I will die when
Leviathan rises
from the wet,

a shadow on shadows,
and asks me her
unanswerable question.

NARCISSUS AT THE PHARMACY

Now that I am sick,
I have become
so important
to myself.

My reflection in every
surface, no matter
how marbled or matte.

My story swelling
like a Magic Eye
in every page I read.

The world is ending, yes,
but am I not a world?

A country, at least, to the
lives that live within me—
the bodies and antibodies.
Custodians and usurpers.

And like a tyrant
bedbound with gout,

I have been waking
in the witching hour,
obsessing over legacy

and who will inherit
my debts and vendettas.

Ach, the moon is such
a lousy prescription.
Such a queasy pill.

And the river is such
an inattentive orderly.

This soil has such a
bitter bedside manner.
So unsteady a hand to hold.

Atop this crematory heap
of suffocating supplicants,

as the hot ash finds
the last of the Minoans,
scuttled in fields of saffron,

I beg and I weep and I rage:

But what about me?
Beautiful me?
What will become,
after all, of me?

THE METAPHOR GAME

In the MRI machine,
I play the metaphor game
that whispered me some courage
through the many dooms of childhood.

I am a loaded torpedo in a submarine. No—
I am a treasure in a shipwrecked hull. No—
I am a moray eel in a cavern of coral. No.

I am a deep-water creature. I am hideous
but unwitnessed. Immortal-esque. It is my
bioluminescence that populates these X-rays.

In this metal clack, in this backless gown
with its new layers of nudity, I remember
my favorite part of the nightmare: when

you know one thing signifies another thing,
and you don't know how you know, but
you know. It's impossible to explain.

I am the Christ of the Abyss. No—I am
a Fresnel lens revolving in a lighthouse. No—
I am a bubble, widening, rising to the surface.

UTOPIA

A secret place to vomit
in the hollow of all things—
accessible from anywhere,
instantaneously. With a snap
of my fingers, bookshelves
swivel. Trapdoors unfasten.

My palace of malady.
A scallop-shell citadel
where no one knocks impatiently.
No embarrassing noises
breach the vacuum. No strangers'
after-shavings in the sink.

A secret place to vomit
outfitted for the purpose—
a Muzak of loon calls and sea breeze
weeping from the intercom.
A warmed and sterile basin
at an accessible height

with carpeted kneepads
and a masseuse's face cradle.
Clean shirts unspool from a hands-
free dispenser. A spritz of air
freshener envelops me.
I am minted and watered and new.

A secret place to vomit
when my body revolts
or revolts against me. I emerge
as though from a Narnian
wardrobe—no time has passed.
No one asks if I'm all right.

SOCIAL STUDIES, PT. 1

•

All my friends
are so depressed.

And I'm the other thing
they have in common.

•

I trust charisma
in none of its forms.

•

I would never have considered
    that I was an asshole
if people hadn't kept telling me
    that I was an asshole.

For that, perhaps,
I am grateful.

•

In the end, we all become
whoever was nice to us
when we were fifteen.

•

All my friends hate
small talk. But me,
good God, I love it.

That hesitant tango,
its electric potentials.

How a gesture,
      barely there,
could become the fulcrum
      on which the everything
between us wobbles.

With someone who loves you,
there's nothing at stake.

The talk can not
get small enough
      for me.

•

The final frontier
is another person.

•

It is narcissism, I suppose,
to see so many ghosts.

Just because I miss them
doesn't mean they're dead.

•

To all my pseudo-friends,
      my semi-friends,
the friends with one foot
      out the door:

Keep up the act.
It's working wonders
in ways you can't imagine.

CAUTION!

Nothing is safe ! All this time ! our breastplates ! were aluminum foil ! These balustrades ! are Styrofoam props ! Do not lean ! They can be blown ! over and apart ! by a medium ! wind ! Watch ! The ice is warm ! and cracking ! Tap it with your heel ! Gently ! Gentler ! Hold this stemware ! to the light : tiny killers ! swim inside ! This lifeboat ! whistles ! through a duct-taped *x* ! The lighthouse ! keeper ! is not on our side ! Can't you smell it ? Weather is coming ! When we capsize ! take my hand ! though it's oily ! and I'm weak ! Can't you feel it ? Your skin is damp ! tissue paper ! It can be rolled ! up like a sleeve ! And underneath ! your body ! is a rusting ! weave of gears ! All paper clips ! and glue ! Your threads ! are taut ! Nearly ! snapping ! Watch your step ! This whole ! fucking place ! is a gauntlet ! There are bear traps ! in the cabbage patches ! Landmines ! in the dance floor ! Caution ! Can't you hear ? this ogre snoring ? All is folly ! All is foible ! All is out to get us ! I am so sorry ! really, to preach ! this worry gospel ! But all the worst things ! I can imagine ! are real.

BURDEN OF CARE

I have steamed the fucking spinach
without a single flake of salt
and I have let it dissolve
like wet sand and jellyfish
in the grottos of my tonsils.

I have circled the block
in my embarrassment of sneakers.
Swinging again this cowbell
of pharmaceuticals,
I am circling the block.

I alarm myself early,
even on the weekends.

Yes, I've been doing the stretches.
Yes, I've been wearing the brace.

Of course I've kept a journal
of all my aches and visions.

The doctor and I
have been playing mancala
with pills and their milligrams
and, oh, their interactions.

The doctor is winning.

Expect to gain weight.
There will always be pain.
The trick is in the maintenance.

And perhaps I'll be all right.
The wisest and the wellest
all swear by their routines.

But I don't want to think
about my body anymore.

I want to learn Spanish
for real and for good.

I want to watch all day
      for waterbirds
and run to tell my wife.

SUICIDAL IN PARADISE

When I see driftwood, I think *shipwreck*.
And I don't think I'm alone. Here,
in the company of a hundred sunburned shoulders,
I'm a freak amid this fitness.

An animal is at its most vulnerable
when its belly is prone, and seagulls
have been circling my stress-sweat for hours.

So I button up my bowling shirt
and wave away a mai tai.

I scour the beach for horseshoe
crab shells fragrant with roe;

for neglected SOSs of pebbles and pearls
and for the skeletons that spelled them out.

But all I find are thriving bodies. Volleyballers,
frolickers, bare heels combing the sand
for the sharp and rusty corners of treasure chests.

Haven't they noticed those overhead coconuts
and the measly feathered hooks on which they sway?

Haven't they heard you can't drink seawater?
That we'll have to survive by sucking on fish eyes?

An island is a prone place, all belly.
A dungeon under siege.

And I don't know how to love
a thing I didn't pay or suffer for.
It's a virtue where I come from.

There are parasols here for skyborne cancers,
blankets to stay the hurricane breeze.
They make repellants for repellant things
and currents to punish the reckless.

It's night now, no lifeguard on duty.
The blackness is spattered with galaxies.
And what bats at those tombstone buoys?
What awaits me in that brackish undertow?

RED-EYE

Crying on the red-eye,
intercontinental, a precipice
above the precipitating heap-clouds.

E.T. went home, and I knew it was coming.

But something about that depressurizing
headspace, those inhalers of chardonnay . . .

Something about the little silver screen
that comes and goes at certain angles . . .

I don't want to wake the stranger
who's been drooling on my shoulder
since the sun rose over Senegal.

And I couldn't bear to face
the flight attendant in this state.
She has been so patient and tidy
in her immaculate lavender neckerchief.

You can see the ocean from up here—
breaching bodies, frigate ships,
their intersecting wakes.

E.T. says *come*. Elliott says *stay*.
And then they both say *ouch*.

II. SO LONG MY BOY AND BE CAREFULL

SURGERIES

When the surgeons land their spaceships,
they will find you are a world.

Inchoate, volcanic, still
battered by asteroids,

then breathable, bubbling,
brushed by frontier.

And when the surgeons lay their chisels
in the divots of your skin,
they will find you are a geode

whose angles run wild and violet
in your desiccated hollows.

When the surgeons drop their lines,
they will find you are an ocean

of fringing reefs and woven stipes;
forgotten anchors snared in the holdfast.

They will discover the color dulls
the deeper they sink.

And were the surgeons just to knock,
they would find you are a room

where the dogs are ostensibly
prohibited from the couch

and the upright piano
has a dead middle F.

They would find you are a room

with a little bronze Buddha,
his belly distressed,

and a clock that doesn't work
but was your mother's.

THE MUSEUM OF HOSPITAL ART

I swear I could spend weeks
at the Museum of Hospital Art.

I am not immune to the soothing
of a pelican descending at sunset.

Nor even to a lighthouse in graphite,
Fresnel lens trained south upon the isthmus.

I am not above a pastel brook.
I do not miss the shadows.

And I could practically live
in this Palliative Wing,

losing myself in the orbit of these murals,
pacing for hours in acrylic glacial pines.

And I have learned to love the textiles
donated by the synagogue. I have
made peace with the tulips.

And I could spend the rest of my long life
in this one room in particular, mixed-
media, a seasonal installation.

In this one room, this pageant
of wires and ready-made Jell-O,

where Rachel Maddow plays on mute
and wind chimes ring from the monitors,

I am a model. Here, I'm on display.
A Polaroid portrait from my toddlerhood.
To the left, I am older, accepting my diploma.

And I could stare forever,
this one forever night,
at this one forever sculpture,

cracked ceramic skin, a forearm
spackled in purple nebulae.

In its silent, abstract way, I swear
there must be something
it's trying to say.

TEN THINGS I LOVE ABOUT VISITING YOU IN THE HOSPITAL

1. Free Wi-Fi.

2. The slow and glassy fountains
   ever *shush*ing in the atrium.

3. Strangers give you space.
   No one's here on holiday.

4. Urns on urns of coffee
   like a ruptured vein of oil.

5. You aren't dead yet.

6. The player piano
   haunted in the lobby. You
   don't see those anymore.

7. Plenty of time with family.
   It's been too long, you know.
   We have each other's numbers.

8. Plastic-wrapped cookies
   and donuts and scones.

9. I know this is selfish, but if I,
   myself, start dying, I'll be glad
   that I was here, so near
   these sterile implements
   of endurance and revival.
   So blessed by the expert hands
   of strangers. Bless the strangers
   who can watch a person
   writhe and weep and piss
   and shut that suffering in

the filing cabinets of their hearts.
Goddamn me to hell, I
wouldn't know where to start.

10. Plastic birds of paradise
 never rotting by the windows.

WATCHING *THE FELLOWSHIP OF THE RING* WITH GRANDPA NEAR THE END OF HIS LIFE

No, they're not kids. They're called hobbits.
And this isn't England. It's the Shire. No,
not Yorkshire. It's not England, I said. It's
nowhere on the British Isles whatsoever.
It's called Middle-earth. It's an imaginary—
Yes, I know they have British accents.
It's supposed to remind you a little bit
of rural England right before the war.
But don't get too caught up in the history.
It's fantasy. No, they're not a couple. I mean—
they might be. But that doesn't matter.
All you need to know for our purposes is
that they love each other and war is coming.
And war will trail its webs of lack behind them.
All that wandering, the bed-wetting dreams.
Hardtack rotting in the storerooms. The
smell of damp and greening injuries.
And everyone will be sorted on a palette
of violence. The hobbits will come to hear
the thrumming dead in mounds of rubble.
To taste the blood in all their pub songs.
And men who love each other will have to
learn to say it out loud. Yes, I know that
some elves are small. But these ones are tall.
They're exhausted with all this decay and
they're leaving for the Undying Lands. No—
I don't know what that means, either.

SO LONG MY BOY AND BE CAREFULL

Found Documents from My Grandfather's Desk

1. *Letter from My Great-Grandmother, Bessie, to the Captain of the Illinois State Militia, Dated April 24, 1941*

Dear Captain C _____ :

On February 28th, 1941, my son, Haskell B _____ , apparently was registered in Company M, 132nd Infantry, 2nd Regiment, in the Illinois State Militia.

My son is only thirteen years of age, becoming fourteen years old on June 6, 1941. When I learned of his registration on his return home that evening I immediately notified officers of this company giving them his correct age and stating that he never had my consent to register.

My son's father and I are divorced and I have sole custody of my son, and I insist that his registration be corrected to show his correct age and that he be discharged or his registration cancelled.

The officers of the company advised me almost two months ago that the correction would be made and that I would receive a discharge from Springfield in about thirty days. To date we have not received these papers and consequently I am writing you asking that you give this matter your immediate attention.

I will appreciate your doing everything possible to have this error corrected and the discharge papers—or whatever papers are necessary—issued.

I understand that the Company meets on Tuesday nights at the Broadway Armory, and I will be there next Tuesday to see you and I will bring along the birth certificate showing my son's correct age.

Thanking you for any aid and assistance that you may be able to render to me, I am

      Yours very truly,
          Bessie B _____

BRAVER

I thought I would be braver
should a rogue wave find our ship.
I thought I'd dash through flooding cabins,
scooping bodies from the wreckage.

I thought I would be braver,
like my grandfather was brave.
And my anchor, hooked unflummoxed
against the reeling tide.

I thought I would be brave, at least,
where bravery means tenderness.
Should a grieving cheek land on my chest,
I thought I would hold steady.

I was a brave teenager.
Even braver as a child.
Those rocks I hopped were slippery.
And such a fall beneath them.

THE WEIGHT

of a wheelchair works out the hammering muscles,
the handsaw muscles. I don't know what they're called,
but I've noticed them expanding and defining
their veins like soil in the rain.

It's art as well as exercise, the speed and force and angles.
You want to be gentle, but there are hills
to be conquered. Gravel and ice
and the metal under doors.

It's amazing, in this Anthropocene, how one of us strengthens
while the other one weakens. Our machines
and bodies, braided together,
mutual parasites.

There is genius here: Just as we approach
        the pallbearing season,
our forearms, once more, become fit for the task.

AFTERLIFE

When you die,
you become money
and you become the things
that stand for money.
And the people you love
will be haunted by the
many-taloned ghost of your
money or—if your money
was goodly—swept from
danger in its dust cloud.
And when you come to
visit in their sleep or stupor,
you will speak to them
in the language of money,
which nobody speaks,
but everyone understands.
And when they find you,
dangled in an old
and mothballed closet,
they will hold your money
against their money, and
some new and hybrid money
will make itself matter
and make itself feeling
and in time become
a shade. A watermark,
your fossil. And grief
is the telltale clacking
of an abacus. And grief
is a séance by spreadsheet.
And when you are born,
you are money come back
to claim a body. Money
learning how to love.

SO LONG MY BOY AND BE CAREFULL

Found Documents from My Grandfather's Desk

2. *Stack of Postcards from My Grandfather to His Mother and Sister from the Academy, Undated*

•

Hello Ma
I am having a swell time.
Haskell

•

Hello Ma E.T.C.
That duffle bag is swell.
There is too much to write
and too little time

•

Dear Mom
I am fine. The water is swell.
Did you have to address all the
post cards to yourself? It's more
fun telling that writing so I'll save it.
Haskell

•

Hello Ma
I am still having a swell time.
Haskell

To Stinky Sissy
We are going to the Avon.
Your cute and darling little
brother.

P.S. I hate you

OF MY FICTIONS

The immortal dogs of my fictions,
exhausted from centuries of fetch,
are laid out in puddles of sun

or rummaging for slugs
in the banks of soggy leaves.

It is autumn, and the air
is a bakery of dander and pollen.

It is autumn, and the immortal
dogs of my fictions are sniffing
and digging for ancient wisdoms.

In the bulges of mulch, in the
outstretched hands of children,

there is something I cannot know.

In the oiled rotation of those immortal
hips, amid the unspoiled
brindles and chocolates and merles,

I find a spot to scratch,
and I scratch that spot forever.

Perhaps, if I am kind, one will whimper
by my grave one day, in the shadow
of that eroding masonry, my epitaph
chiseled in the language of dogs.

Freed of leash and muzzle,
with rage and jubilation,

the immortal dogs of my fictions
hunt for squirrels and hummingbirds.

And if they're feeling any pain,
I don't know how I'd know,
but I like to think I would.

WOO

I don't believe in hokum and
I don't believe in woo until,
of course, I do. Like anyone,

I am sometimes desperate and
sometimes grieving and I am
often a constellation of panics.

So I don't believe in claptrap
and I don't believe in bunkum.

Even when my tarot deck
tells me how to love
and when I'll die.

I don't believe in impossibilities.
I'm wary of improbabilities.

I don't actually believe
hurricanes are my fault.

Sure, I might be startled
if a hum I'm sure is passing
traffic manifests in my bedroom.

But ignore me in a foxhole.
I am prey to my survival.

I don't believe in hogwash
and I don't believe in hooey

and I don't believe that magnets
will vacuum up our cancers.

I can't think magically.
I can't believe you'll visit me
through the celestial cellophane.

And I don't believe that love
is a salve for all the suffering,
nor are they comorbidities.

But rather, two shadows,
for a gasp overlapping.

SO LONG MY BOY AND BE CAREFULL

Found Documents from My Grandfather's Desk

3. *Letter to My Grandfather from My Great-Grandfather, Anton, Stationed in Texas, Dated August 16, 1942*

My Dear Boy:

Thank you for your letter of yesterday and I am sorry to say that I have not roped any cattle as yet, but you know me, I might whens the weather gets cooler, for it is hot as hell right now. As to riding horses, that we must do for thats a part of our training or exersize here. I am 1st assistant to examining doctor for Consolidated Bomber Pilots and I am getting only Captain's pay which is about $50 per week but we must pay for our room and board and clothing, laundry etc. so I don't have much money left when I get through paying everybody.

As to the car, you may get in touch with Phil's mother for the car is in her name.

As soon as I get Bessie's permission, I'll send you a picture of me on a horse (mine is white but I dont have to clean it myself). It a mare about 4 year's old and very gentle. It belong to DR Luck who is in charge, but he likes a larger horses so he does'nt use her. This afternoon we may ride on horse backs to "Mineral Wells" a winter resort town about 27 miles from Ft. Worth. In the evening, I am going to see "Eagle Squadron" because we get free ticket from the local U.S.O.

I am sorry to hear that you have a rainy season, for we have had no rain at all, for about 13 weeks. It's so dry here that even snakes congregate at every water hole, and we practice shooting at them. You can take their heads off with a .45 if you aim it good.

Thats all for today because I have to shave and go to mess for dinner, or Ill get nothing to eat. Today we have Southern-fried Chicken and vegetables, and apple pie, and milk.

So long my boy and be carefull.

Your loving Dadd

TWO FATHERS

The first father is sick and the other is mean,
but they require the same sort of care—

mawkish apologies to the front of house.
The sponging up of unspeakable fluids.

You'll shoulder at least one father's weight
like an anchor soldered to a chain of vulgar protests

and damn yourself with desperate bargains
any time he has to take his medicine or eat.

Both fathers must be ferreted away from
first dates but checked on intermittently.

Either could be so easily tipped from sleep
to non-sleep to something like sleep.

All fathers come out even in the wash—
neither will apologize for what he

can't remember and neither will recognize
himself in the red eyes at his bedside.

You will gamble away days of unbearable
length checking off boxes on dire forms,

then forfeit your nights playing Whac-A-Mole
with the worst vermin of your imagination.

This won't be your last dawn spent tilting
vending machines with whichever sibling's left.

This won't be the last time I'll have to
remind you that mean is a kind of sick.

Mean, I repeat, is a kind of sick.

LIFEBED

The dead
surround my lifebed.

They take turns
holding my hand.

They do not know
if I can hear them.

But they are apologizing
and reminiscing and hoping
I am not in too much pain.

The dead
do not agree

about what is to be done
with my body and soul
and money and tchotchkes.

They cannot hear
me screaming.

Is living like sleeping?
they ask. (They
do not remember.)

*Does living feel
like eternity
or like no time at all?*

And, God, I wish
I could answer them.

I have so many answers
on my lifebed
about life.

So many answers
I am damned to forget.

PART 2

THE WELL

I. COHABITATIONS

THE OLD HOUSE

I am back in the old house,
where I kissed no girls
and kissed no boys,

then kissed them all at once,
in a sort of reaping motion,
'round one spun bottle
relieved of its triple sec.

I am back in the old house,
where I loved the dog
who bit my mother often.

And where a starling found
a laceration in the windowsill
and died behind my bed.

I am back in that house.

Where I hid my weed
in a collapsible Death Star
the size of a softball.

I am back in the yard
where every passing ant
was a chance to prove
my mercy or wrath.

And I threatened to run
away forever, which is
a child's way of saying
something unspeakable.

I am back in the old house.
Fist marks in the drywall.

Hoisting plastic crates
heavy with winter purses,
Phillips-heads, brass menorahs
preserved in amber crayon.

There are photographs
of prehistoric aunts
and photocopied terms
of the divorce.

I am back in the old house,
poltergeisted by apologies.

Gremlins of resentment
in the gears of the recliner.

I am back in this pillared maze
where we suffered and rejoiced.

Where I practiced "Purple Haze"
for weeks until, my God,
I thought I really had it.

SOCIAL STUDIES, PT. 2

•

Secret deals are made
on the fire escape.

•

I wish I had a tag
that said, "I'm sick"

and I wish I had a tag
that said, "I'm healthy"

and I wish these tags were sacred
to all you comely minglers.

•

*Don't bring up dictators.
Nobody wants to talk about dictators.
There is no such thing
as a "fun fact" about Stalin.*

•

I am too old and disordered
        for these marathon drugs.

I sicken too easily.

        I am half a life away
from waking on the hardwood

of people who hate me.

•

My least favorite sound
is everyone else sleeping.

•

I am willing to make
so many concessions.

But yes, it would kill me
to put some gel in my hair.

Shoes are for walking.
What good is a pair
I can't get dirty?

It took me decades to learn
I don't have to be beautiful.

God forbid
I forget that now.

•

In retrospect, much
of what I blamed
on my T-shirts

was, after all,
my torso's fault.

•

If the ten people in this room
were the last alive on earth,

eight of us would drink
deep and dance close

and the two remaining wallflowers
would disappear early,
the last of our kind
in separate apartments.

CHICAGO IN WINTER

It is some madness
to fall in love
in Chicago in winter,

when the world becomes
an un-scrapeable windshield

and the snow bolds the branches
      like highlighted text.

When the dumpsters are soldered shut

and mittens have sullied
the holding of hands.

Some new madness to fall in love

at the bookends of the ten-hour
workday, still possessed by the
      echoes of *Jingle Bells*

(and still possessed by all
our other dybbukim besides).

When the buses runneth over
and we insulate with duct tape.

When the river is spotted
by lily pads of green ice.

When the rent and weather conspire
    to a killing spree.

When your hot breath finds my chest
and it feels so much like stealing.

GREEN COUCH

A word about the couch,
with its fiddlehead arms
and lichen upholstery:

It appeared to us years ago,
piecemeal by a dumpster,
and we scurried it, like worker ants,
up a narrow, dusty stairwell.

There is godly satisfaction
in the clicking of wooden slats
and a cushion skating into place.

And you hope your guests won't notice
it can come apart so easily.

Like a galleon in a glass bottle,
you hope it looks like magic.

Take comfort. This couch
has unburdened dozens,
drunken or in transit or in crisis,
of their wakeful encumbrances.

And know that it is jeweled with fluids—
soy sauce and Côtes du Rhône
and bloody noses and so much worse.

It is a second place to occupy
should I become unlovable,
which I often do after too much
time in too little space.

Like a bill into a wallet,
I slip into the tatty divot
that tired backs have worn.

Blades of midday sun, always
the smell of something burning.

This couch is a long, green silence
shared between people in love.

And you should hear the song it sings
when both our weights are lain upon it.

IN A TENT

Two weeks in a tent with Julio,
who I hardly knew, on an isle
in a piney sound, buttered with fog.

There were kayaks in grayscale.
Roots undressed in mudslides
and pressed into our spines.

One night, huddled from a storm,
he mixed us margaritas in his Nalgene
and laid out a little bag for cigarette butts.

Insomniacs in binary orbit, we
stared through the convertible flap
at the rain and the stars—

unyielding and transient bodies
of astonishing chemical breadth,
phasing in and out of eclipse.

We spoke at length about the way
the wireweed and dead-man's-
fingers lingered on our oars;

those precious days when crabbers
passed, honked their klaxons
and waved from the aft.

The stars, he offered, were a kind
of archipelago, insofar as space
could be seen as a kind of sound.

And he asked what I knew about the visitors.

Well, of course you got your Grays,
he said. *Zeta Reticulans. They
do most of the abducting.*

*You've got Reptilians. And Nordics
from the Pleiades. Andromedans:
beings like light on a mirror.*

And in that drumming
of the wind against the tent,
he asked if I was afraid.

TO THE SPIDERS, I WHISPER:

Run away before she sees you!
In a braid of limbs, escape!

Build a secret home inside our home.
Find some wet and wooden abscess.

Feast and breed and live forever.

She is in the next room.
I can hear her playful advance.

Run away and hide and thrive!

She will ask me to kill you.
And I love her, so I will.

INDEFINITELY

My mother, my brother, and me, indefinitely
displaced by black mold and divorce,
safe for a summer in a government building
moated by highways, our fort on a landfill.

Safe, for a spell, blessed
with our potable tap
and the labyrinthine lobby
with its many keys and codes.

We were safe because my mother
checked the mail for anthrax
and would call me out of school
anytime I asked.

Safe because my brother
was only allowed
to shoot me with his BB gun
if he aimed for my butt or legs.

Because my copy of *The Marshall Mathers LP*
was hidden safely in the pillowcase of my beige-
stained Murphy bed, itself a bridge drawn safely
in the wall. Because a secret is a way to be safe.

My mother, scared of stairs,
the tumbling of her body.
My brother, of tornadoes,
the twirling off of his.

The boy next door,
blessed be his Dreamcast,
scared of me, because
he'd never met a Jew before.

And for all I thought of dying, then and even now,
I was only ever scared of having one of my spells
in a crescent of cackling jocks. Anything personal,
really, coming to light in unsympathetic company.

But I felt safe there, indefinitely,
miles away from any devil I knew.
Who could even find us here?
Who would even be looking?

MISE EN PLACE

•

No infinity
and no celestial heat
would soften these beets.

•

Blink and you'll miss it:
I'm tossing the pasta.

Jellyfish tentacles
whipped in the current.

Smoke and stock and
toasted chili flakes.

The garlic at marshmallow tan.

Imagine this wave breaking.
Just imagine my shame.

•

Whatever genius reminds a person
not to touch the scalding pan:
this I do not have and cannot learn.

•

Because I have no garden,
I have a bar. And I tend it
like a garden, with filth
beneath my fingernails.
With a cape of sweat

and the devil in my joints.
With the patience of labor:
that *someday, I swear* . . .

•

I shall not eat bacon
and I shall not eat pork

for the pigs are so beautiful
and their hooves are flamenco.

Because they mourn and play
and *Hey!* so do I. Because

the piglets snore like rising dough and
the old pigs' ears go soft and sagging.

I shall not eat gelatin
and I shall not eat ham

because I'm trying to be
kinder and I'm trying to be
thinner and sometimes I worry

there'd be nothing left of me
if you took away the hungers.

•

The most powerful thing I did all week
was pinch the avocados in the produce aisle
one by one and turn them and *tsk*
and, finding them lacking, go simply without.

•

Deep down, I know
the bay leaf is a placebo,
but the best magicians
believe their own tricks.

•

Because she loves me,
we do not address the
rawness in the center.

She eats it all
and so do I.

•

Somewhere, in all this body,
I must contain a delicacy.

Some sickly sweet, some ambergris,
some rare and piquant cut.

In all this souring, in all this toxic,
find a part to smoke or cure.

You may hate it at first.
Try a little on toast.

•

From the alley, I discover
a stew has been stovetop
for several hours.

Cabbage, I'd swear,
some sausage or offal,
and a whole pine forest
of dill from the windowsill.

I hate the smell of dill,
and especially the taste.

But this isn't about
what I hate.

HALFWAY

I live in half a house.

The foundation was laid
        in the late eighties
and the rest was never finished.

Lattices of lumber
        with Tyvek siding;
wedges of various synthetics.

Small intestine pipework,
        endocrine heating vents;

nervous system haywire, sparks
chirping and fraying at night.

I shower beneath
        the incessant leak
of wheezing aluminum bellows.

        I sleep on a mattress
of exposed rubber-brass springs

and wake each morning with new
surgeries embedded in my back.

        Loose screws manage
        through moccasin and foot.

Stalagmites of sawdust
        and asbestos residue.

    A decapitated spinal staircase.

        I live in half—

Skate rats and addicts
        commingle in my foyer.

Double-daring preteens,
indigent possums.

        The neighbors have seen
my every shameful angle,

and the termites want me gone.

—a house.

        Folks often ask me
what I do when it rains.

        What can I say?

I get wet.

IN FIDELITY

Don't tell my wife,
but I still fall in love
with rock stars.

Like a teenager,
belly to the mattress,
headphones in.

My wife doesn't know,
but I know all the words
and sometimes the chords.

And though I am happy
and happy in love, happy
is not an on/off switch.

And love is not a single track
grooved into a mountainside.

Circling a sponge
around the saucepan,
I am sighing,
headphones in.

I have these shameful fantasies
in which a rock star
finds me beautiful,

even at this age, and
with all of my conditions.

In which they press
a glittered cheek against my cheek,
and another to my wife's,

and the three of us learn together
how any life, loud or soft,
gets drowned out in the mix.

IN QUARANTINE

I'm ashamed of how afraid I am.
I am gluttonous in my fortunes.

But what is love and the home
one grouts about its borders

if not a kind of doomsday bunker?
Are we not always shopping
for a place to die?

I've been struggling to breathe,

so I've deleted all my porn
and the poems I wrote in anger.

I have not found God.
I've abandoned my diet.

Outside there are crickets, a spatter
of cardinals, the neighborhood
labs in all their drooling wisdom.

Inside, we have ridden the pendulum
of bickering and forgiveness and we've
come out twisted like creeping vines,
hypnotized, bound by the understory.

We have been hunching over jigsaws
and sunning ourselves in *Doctor Who*.

And like the TARDIS, this apartment
is bigger on the inside. Rooms
are the dreams of rooms.

THE NEW HOUSE

Could this room, this massive room
with the undulant hardwood
and dubious electric,

could this be the altar upon which
hors d'oeuvres are sacrificed?

Could this room hold all our love
and all the thrumming pulses
of all the distant friends

who could, someday, migrate our way,
a check mark in the distance?

Could this roof, this clef of gutters,
in all its damp hypotenuses,

could it catch the overhead evils
and guide them to the dirt,
a pachinko of malady?

Could this room, this tiny room,
more radiator than wall,
contain some ancient
brimming coffer?

My love, we both suffered
in our palatial cribs.

Like child monarchs, slouched
and sickly and crowded
by friendlessness.

But what if we nest in these
midwestern tresses to find
that all our busy sorrows

were but a shelf of insufficient depth,
a window angled toward no light,

a sink that could be clogged
with just a crumb of grit?

What kind of evergreen beauty
might lichen up these plaster walls

if we put the green couch
right here, like this?

II. THE GOLEM

BETTER

I've been fooled before,
but I think I'm getting better.

I think I'm breathing deeper
and I think I'm seeing farther
and fewer situations lately
call for drastic measures.

This might not be related,
but I think I'm getting taller.
I am discovering the dusty
tops of cabinets. There are
bald spots I hadn't noticed
on people I thought I knew.

There is no way to prove this,
but I think I can leave my house
again, more often and for longer.
I am open to muddier traversals.

I will have to account
for this gap in my résumé.
I will have to reevaluate
the boundaries of my wardrobe.

It will be hard to explain
how bad it used to get.
It's always been hard,
but I think it might get harder.

I could be imagining things,
but all around me, neon
lights are dimming.

Someone's cleared the rubble.
The sirens, as it happened,
meant no harm at all.

Knock on wood. Grain of salt.
Could it be that all this time
there was half a solution
to half the problem?

My madness is modest,
my pain is Advillable.

I am rolling down
the long sock of death.

And when I imagine
something beautiful,
something beautiful
contains me.

TWO SONS

In her dresser drawer,
my mother kept

one book about raising
a gifted son

and one book about raising
a troubled son.

With mercy first,
I never told my brother

what I found whirring in
that engine of our childhoods.

I keep this secret
among my many gifts.

No one wants to be,
after all, the troubled son.

BUS STOPS

I.

I do not love myself
when I chase after the bus
in scuffed-up Chucks
one size too small.

Especially after midnight,
with a day's pay in split tips
crimped against my chest
like a paisley pocket square.

Friends, forgive me
my dismissal of the upturned palms
that wait for ten lifetimes
beneath those barely heated lamps.

I am just like anyone else—
paranoid and in a terrible rush.
And I just want what everyone wants—
to be left alone with my headphones in,

unmolested by errant elbow
or overzealous conversation.
Not at work, not at home.
This time is mine and it is precious.

II.

A shrink once told me
that it's a sickness
to love and fear a thing at once.

But all these melancholy
strangers, so very close together,
slowly going mad
in the same cardinal direction!

All their eavesdropping,
their tremoring knees!

In this lanyard of tragedy,
this heaving rain-stick
of swollen gums and joints.

In this caravan of local itinerants—
our motion and our stillness.

Of course I am afraid of them.
Of course I love you all.

III.

This is summer camp come roundabout, these
glacial sunrises spent waiting for the bus.

Sometimes it's early, sometimes it's late, sometimes
it passes me altogether, as a mudslide might a root.

No one goes walking so early in the day.
Not beneath this gray and salmon sky.

Not while street cats cuddle by the exit ramps
and corner stores are shackled in their cells.

It's not like me to trust a thing this much—
to ferry my body, alive and on time,

to the dreamland of work, paralyzed and
in endless locomotion, selfless and indebted.

A little girl, unaccompanied, breathes on the glass
and traces a curly-haired stick figure in the condensation.

When I was her age, I sat in the back with my Game Boy.
I said cruel things I didn't understand or mean.

And I pretended not to notice my mother,
eternal on the curbside, smiling and
waving and worrying to death.

IV.

I do not love—in fact I hate—
when the bus starts moving
while I'm still standing

and I have to hook and stomp
my way from strap to strap
and rod to rod like a
courier in a sandstorm.

But that's the thing about buses:

You're standing still
and you're standing still
and just like that,
you're moving.

HEROIN, PT. 1

I am a child, and the adults
are trying to explain heroin.

These are the Tamagotchi years.
The internet is inchoate.

And the adults are *umming*
and *erming* about heroin.

They are not the stewards of a
psychopharmacological lexicon.

They are bureaucrats
and they are grieving.

I am a child, and the adults
are straining to explain

a medicine you don't need, I guess,
but then you need it really bad.

More than food and more than sleep
and even more than family.

I am a child. I have not begun
to understand the body

as a brace of rabbits battling
over pine needles in the winter.

Or the interwoven chutes
and funnels of a water park.

(Children splashing, lifeguards
whistling, vulgar solvents
vanishing in acid.)

I am a child. I struggle with division.

And even I can tell the adults
are yoked by secret wisdom.

Like actors bombing side by side,
like accomplices flop-sweating
in separate interrogation rooms,

there are cracks in the telling
and they're desperate to patch them.

But it does me no good to
grapple with the grammar of

something that makes you feel better
but then it makes you feel worse

and it makes you feel better
and eventually you die.

I have not fathomed lack
nor reckoned with regret.

I have not come to know the
conscience as a turning prism.

And I don't know what to picture
when I picture a bliss worth dying for.

Something to do with puppies,
I guess, or autopsying ice cream
from a carapace of butterscotch.

Or floating face up in salt water,
my grandfather's hand
a pillar at my spine.

A CITY WITHOUT MONEY

I think I would be lonely
in a city without money.

To not be known by name
at any taqueria, to never wave
good morning between those
effervescing vats of aguas frescas.

It's not an insignificant thing,
I think, to pat the staffy
who guards the bar.

To shoot Malört on
a mutual dare, to relish
the *ſwift* of darts implanting.

I have taken my wages
and whatever time is left
and I have mashed it all
into a theater of love.

How hard, really,
could I be to hold?

My head has been so
delicately shampooed by
the barber with the ear tattoos.

And how hard, really,
could I be to get to know?

I am privy to the traumas
of the laundrywoman.
Together we have wept.

I think I would be lonely
and I think I would be hungry

because this is how we eat
in a city with money. This
is how we eat each other.

MATRYOSHKA

My baby has (a baby—
a porcelain bauble (baked
into a king cake. An infant
(infinitesimal, breathless, mostly
heartbeat. (And arching
in its (paunch, a child with (child, itself
distended with the water-
(weight of triplets, (quadruplets,
an uncountable bounty
clustered (like drupelets. Branching
fractals of little hands.
(Umbilical bouquets (and
tessellated placentae.
An infinity (mirror mosaicked
in ultrasound. In dreams
(my babies and their
babies (overtake me
like ants. Listen
(to their echoing chambers.
From (a distance, I watch (the excess of
my body (go elastic—
spread thin (like floodwater,
butter pat, ball bearings
fallen (on the floor.
What humbling (gust
has so unmoored
the (spokes from my seed-head?
What (futures root
in the fallout?

THE GOLEM

It hurts to make
and it hurts to be made
of this blood-red, blood-wet clay.

To feel your knuckles smear
to paste against the hand-hold,
the toe-hold. To plummet
back down into the riverbed.

It hurts to return to where
you came from, no matter
what became of it or you.

It hurts to submerge
and hurts to emerge, sopping,
moldable—a chandelier
of bubbles and foam.

It hurts to be tainted and hurts
to be pure and hurts to glance
back at the impure calligraphy
you've left squirming in the mikveh.

It hurts to be used
and it hurts to be useless
and it hurts to get used
to anything hurting.

I don't think I'll have time
to love my body before it sets,
dries out, shatters.

It would kill me to swim
in the murkening river of my life
before it stagnates, evaporates,

transfers its name
to the valley it leaves behind.

CLOSING UP SHOP

I am closing up shop
at the end of the world.

I am switching off
the *Open* sign.

I am sweeping up the leaves
and I am sweeping up the trees
and I am picking from the bristles
all the sparrows' nests and tire swings.

I am sopping up the marshes
with a bucket and a mop.

Sponging lichen
off the mountainsides.

I am draining the lakes
and squeegeeing the sky.

And when all the rest is done,
I am the brilliance in the alleyway.

The steward of all this waste.

Mine is the fist that raps
the lids of dumpsters
to shoo away the rats.

Mine are the palms
collapsing cardboard boxes.

Mine is the math that parts
the tips from profit.

Mine is the time and the body.

And mine is the wrist
that twists the key.

WORK

If work is not beautiful,
then I am not beautiful,
and I was never beautiful
in all those heaving hours.

And this home
was never beautiful,
nor any of its furnitures.

Not a bite we cooked here.
Not the laughter in the ducts.

And if work is not beautiful,
then a debt is just a promise
to be kept or maybe not.

And the having, after all,
is just a lullaby of having.

And if work is not beautiful,
then what dark matter
is absent in our stillness?

For even in my sleep,
I sense that I am ugly.

Even in my sleep,
I know to be ashamed.

HATING MY BABY

I'm afraid I'll hate my baby,
since we don't choose what we hate.

And I've always hated the things
that wake me, screaming, in the night.

Whatever keeps me cooped up, sexless,
yoked to the rotation of an engine I can't stop.

These are the things I hate,
and I'm afraid I'll hate my baby.

Because I'm always blaming
the slippery-goddamned-brittle-
fucking plates I shatter on the floor.

Because I hate the heat and I hate crowds
and I hate capitalism and my baby
will want to go to Disney World.

Because I mostly hate my frailty
and I'd hate to meet a frailer me
and I likewise hate the dybbuk
who slinkies down the family.

I don't want to hate my baby.
I don't want to hate anything.

Because I often come to love
the things I used to hate.

And by that time, they've mastered
life without my love.

I'm afraid I'll hate my baby because
that would be the wrong way to feel.

And look at me: I've been feeling
the wrong ways all my life.

DAVID COMES HOME

David, I don't know how to say this,
but I didn't think you'd make it.

For I have met this particular Goliath,
naked in the shuckling pews of wheat.

And in his shadow, I have seen
the rubble of other kings,

cudgeled and rotted and stacked so high
they cast a shadow of their own.

David, you are king, with a lyre and a sling.

But you are also a foal,
lacquered in your mother's blood,
quavering to stand upon this alien loam.

You are king, you are kind,
you are true in song and violence.

But you are bodiced by a body
and the body is the part that errs.

David, forgive me, but I mourned you
in your absence.

For I have been to the Valley of Elah.

I have plucked those ticks and burs
from the thongs of my sandals.

And I'm not always sure
I made it back myself.

But David, my king, even if
we're haunting the same mirage,

raise that bloody bust colossal.
Raise it like a cello bow.

Make us see its sun-dried eyes,
its dangling beard of gore.

I'd share any well for drinking.
Any well for drowning.

I'd follow you in vengeance
and I'd follow you in song.

To the hilts of other champions,
however cruel and towering.

To the crumbling garrets
of temples besieged.

To whichever home you claim as yours
when the warring finds it loves you.

ACKNOWLEDGMENTS

First and foremost, I'd like to thank my wife, Lily, for filling all our time and space together with flowers and poetry. She's in each of these poems, including the ones I wrote before I met her, and this book would have been impossible ten times over without her.

I'd also like to thank some of the many people who have helped me grow creatively and professionally. That includes the faculty and staff at Cornell College, with particular thanks to Glenn Freeman and Steven Sacks. Thanks, as well, to the faculty and staff at New York University's MFA program in Paris, with particular thanks to my advisers, Catherine Barnett, Mark Doty, Nick Laird, and Matthew Rohrer. Thanks to the passionate folks at Tupelo Press, especially to Kristina Marie Darling, and to the supportive team at W. W. Norton, including Mary Dudley.

Thank you to the editors and staff members of the journals and digital formats in which some of these poems first appeared. Thank you to everyone who read and commented on these poems or this manuscript while it was still in progress, with special thanks to Jason Storms for his essential insights. Thanks to Marci Washington for the gorgeous cover art and Mike Corrao for the vivid design. Thank you to Eduardo C. Corral for believing in the book and opening this door. And thank you to my two brilliant editors at Autumn House Press, Christine Stroud and Mike Good, for bringing out the best in the project.

I'd also like to thank my friends for inspiring and forgiving me so many times over the years. Thanks, as well, to my family, particularly my mother, Barbara, my father, Phil, and my siblings, Ami, Danny, and Michael. I'm sorry I never let you read my poetry before. And although my grandfather Charles and grandmother Elaine were never able to see this book come to fruition, they poured their whole hearts into its creation. Thanks to our beloved dog and daughter, Charlie, for making sure I get off the couch and laugh.

I take none of you, and none of this, for granted.

With love,
AI

PREVIOUS WINNERS OF THE AUTUMN HOUSE PRESS RISING WRITER PRIZE

Half-Lives by Lynn Schmeidler,
selected by Matt Bell

Given by Liza Katz Duncan,
selected by Donika Kelly

The Gardens of Our Childhoods by John Belk,
selected by Matthew Dickman

Myth of Pterygium by Diego Gerard Morrison,
selected by Maryse Meijer

In the Antarctic Circle by Dennis James Sweeney,
selected by Yona Harvey

The Gutter Spread Guide to Prayer by Eric Tran,
selected by Stacey Waite

Luxury, Blue Lace by S. Brook Corfman,
selected by Richard Siken

The Drowning Boy's Guide to Water by Cameron Barnett,
selected by Ada Limón

NEW AND FORTHCOMING FROM AUTUMN HOUSE PRESS

I Have Not Considered Consequences: Short Stories by Sherrie Flick

Rodeo by Sunni Brown Wilkinson
Winner of the 2024 Donald Justice Poetry Prize,
selected by Patricia Smith

Bigger: Essays by Ren Cedar Fuller
Winner of the 2024 Autumn House Nonfiction Prize,
selected by Clifford Thompson

The Great Grown-up Game of Make-Believe by Lauren D. Woods
Winner of the 2024 Autumn House Fiction Prize,
selected by Kristen Arnett

self-driving by Betsy Fagin
Winner of the 2024 Autumn House Poetry Prize,
selected by Kazim Ali